A Brief Overview of the Christian Endeavor Society

Brian C. Hull

ISBN: 9781621719397 (print), 9781621719106 (digital), 9781621719113 (kindle)

A Brief Overview of the Christian Endeavor Society.
By Brian C. Hull.
First Fruits Press, ©2019

Digital version at http://place.asburyseminary.edu/christianendeavorbooks/53

For all other uses, contact:
First Fruits Press
B.L. Fisher Library
Asbury Theological Seminary
204 N. Lexington Ave.
Wilmore, KY 40390
http://place.asburyseminary.edu/firstfruits

Hull, Brian C. (Brian Clifford)
 A brief overview of the Christian Endeavor Society / Brian C. Hull. – Wilmore, KY : First Fruits Press, ©2019.

  55 pages : illustrations, portraits ; cm.

  ISBN: 9781621719397 (paperback)
  ISBN: 9781621719106 (uPDF)
  ISBN: 9781621719113 (Mobi)
  OCLC: 1088727934

  1. International Society of Christian Endeavor. 2. United Society of Christian Endeavor. I. Title.

  BV1426.H84 2019

Cover design by Jon Ramsay

asburyseminary.edu
800.2ASBURY
204 North Lexington Avenue
Wilmore, Kentucky 40390

First Fruits
THE ACADEMIC OPEN PRESS OF ASBURY SEMINARY

First Fruits Press
The Academic Open Press of Asbury Theological Seminary
204 N. Lexington Ave., Wilmore, KY 40390
859-858-2236
first.fruits@asburyseminary.edu
asbury.to/firstfruits

Table of Contents

A young photograph of Rev. Francis E. Clark, the Congregational pastor who founded the Christian Endeavor Movement in his parsonage parlor in Portland, Maine in 1881 with 57 young people. Christian Endeavor was the first Christian youth organization, and Clark would become known as the "Father of Youth Ministry." Born in Canada and orphaned at age seven, he was raised by his maternal uncle, Rev. Edward Warren Clark, and would adopt the name of Clark in his honor.

Founding of Christian Endeavor

It was a bitterly cold day in Williston, Maine, with snow covering the ground and icicles hanging from the eaves, but still around sixty young people showed up that Sunday night in February 1881. This was the regular youth meeting in the home of the pastor, Dr. Francis E. Clark.

> "After a little general conversation as to the importance of starting right, or working for the Church, and of showing one's colours for Christ on all occasions, Dr. Clark with, as later admitted, 'a good deal of hesitation,' produced a constitution, the germs of which had lain in his mind for a long while, but which he had written out for the first time that day. It proposed that the society should be called the 'Williston Young People's Society of Christian Endeavour.' Its object was declared to be 'to promote the earnest Christian life among its members, to increase their mutual acquaintance, and to make them more useful in the service of God.'"[1]

There would be specific membership in the society with officers and three committees: the prayer meeting committee, the social committee, and the lookout committee. The expectation for the prayer meeting was that every member attend each meeting and "that each one will take some part however slight in the meeting."[2] The group did not expect this. They had never even heard of anything like this. When Clark finished reading a deathly silence fell.

---

1 Clark, *Christian Endeavor in All Lands*, 35-36.

2 Clark, *Memories of Many Men in Many Lands : An Autobiography*, 85.

The Christian Endeavor Movement spread rapidly through the United States and Canada, as this early image of a Christian Endeavor society in Nome, Alaska, dated June 28, 1915 attests. By 1906, there were over four million members in 67,000 societies worldwide.

From the Papers of the International Society of Christian Endeavor in the Archives and Special Collections of B.L. Fisher Library, Asbury Theological Seminary, Wilmore, Kentucky.

Clark had already tried many different activities and programs to attract young people to Christ and the church. Some had started well, but all had failed. When Clark had drafted the constitution early that afternoon and showed it to Mrs. Clark, she had expressed some hesitation at first. The two were so engrossed in the conversation about young people that afternoon that Mrs. Clark's cookies she had been preparing for that night were forgotten in the oven and burnt. Now, at the moment of offering this opportunity of actively serving Christ and the church, there was hesitation. Dr. Clark had to wonder if this would be another failure.

After some time of silence, two of the adult leaders present started encouraging some of the young people to step forward, assuring them that the requirements were not too difficult and were attainable. Then the movement started, "One by one the young men and women affixed their names to the document, a few more minutes were spent in conversation, a closing prayer was offered and a hymn sung, and the young people went out into the frosty night to their homes, with many a merry 'Good-night,' 'Good night,' to each other; and the first society of Christian Endeavor was formed."[3]

The young people had all signed the covenant. But Clark had to be wondering if this would really work or if it would be another failed attempt in the growing list. Would this society of young people move the young people of his church to action? Would this help young people grow in their faith? Would this empower them to become active in building the Church? Little could he have known then that this first society would become a global movement with over five million members covering the planet.

Pastors like Dr. Clark, all over the world, were trying to find a way to reach young people for Christ and connect them to the church. During the late 1870's and early 1880's there was a period where older children or young adults were no

---

3 Clark, *Christian Endeavor in All Lands*, 41.

longer finding their place in the church. Sunday Schools of the day focused on teaching children up through when they would typically have finished school at the age of 13. Thus there was a gap between when most churches accepted people to membership at age 17 and when they finished Sunday School.[4] This in-between time was also one where many young people were being tempted with the growing entertainments of society. The result was that many young people were becoming marginal in their faith and church participation, or worse yet, leaving the church altogether.

There were many attempts by many pastors to lure young people into the church and to challenge them to commit to Christ. Most of them revolved around entertainment or short-term revival services.

> "However, the failure of lawn-tennis, of pink teas, and Christmas trees, and summer picnics to strengthen the church and develop the religious life of the young people soon made themselves self-evident; and these many and varied failures were not the least important means of preparing the Christian world for an organization which should plant itself firmly and unequivocally on the basis of service for others for Christ's sake."[5]

Like most churches and pastors, Clark and his church, were focused on what they could do for the young people and how it could win them for Christ, rather than on how it could get them to *serve* Christ and the church.

In wrestling with this youth problem, Clark was significantly influenced by what he saw in Scripture as an explicit valuing of children. For Clark, Christ and Scripture called for the church to prioritize children and to see their training as one of the church's primary purposes. "How to change this state of affairs; how to provide some natural outlet for these young energies; how to furnish appropriate work which should not be

---

4 Springhall, "Building Character in the British Boy: The Attempt to Extend Christian Manliness to Working-Class Adolescents, 1880-1914.," 55.

5 Clark, *Christian Endeavor in All Lands*, 29.

merely playing at work but actually accomplishing something for Christ and the Church, was the great problem of the hour."[6] Clark believed that young people could make a commitment to Christ on their own and that they could grow up in the church committed to Christ. This represents a significant shift in the mindset of the American church especially as it dealt with adolescents. This belief in young people led to a vision of doing ministry *with* young people.

---

6 Clark, *World Wide Endeavor : The Story of the Young People's Society of Christian Endeavor, from the Beginning and in All Lands,* 55.

Christian Endeavor appealed to young people for its combination of Christian service and wholesome entertainment. This image is dated 1914 on the *Robert Fulton* (a Hudson River side-wheel steamer), with the caption "Three Thousand Endeavorers Afloat." Most likely this was an entertainment for the New York Union of Christian Endeavor.

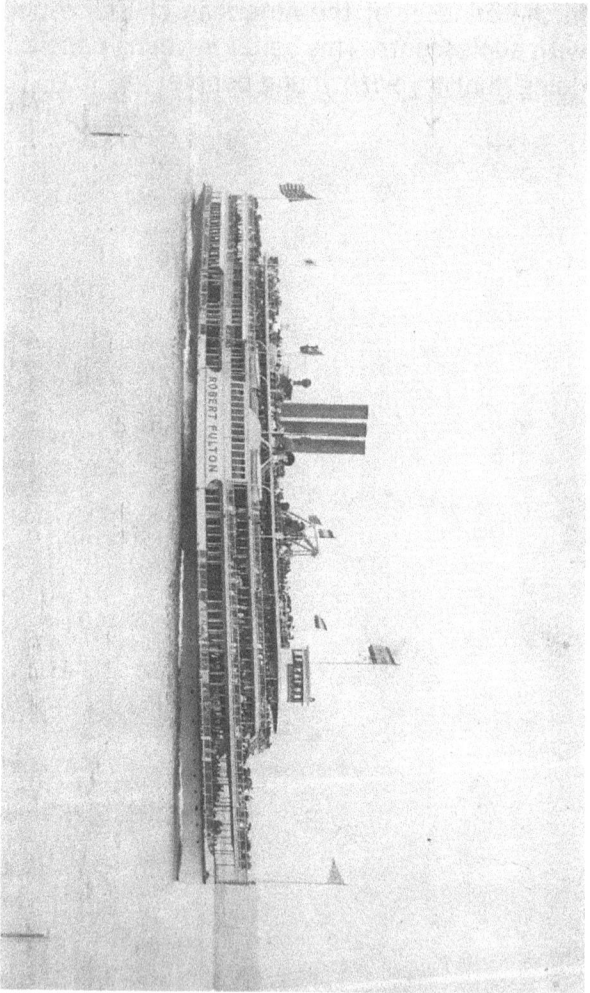

From the Papers of the International Society of Christian Endeavor in the Archives and Special Collections of B.L. Fisher Library, Asbury Theological Seminary, Wilmore, Kentucky.

Organization of Christian Endeavor

It starts on the principle that a child, through the influence of the Spirit of God, may become a Christian very early. It proceeds upon the principle that he needs special watchfulness, care and training to make him strong and serviceable in the household of God. Account for it as we may, there has been a sad lack in the home training and the church training of young Christians. The lack has not been so much in the line of instruction as in the line of practice, and earnest Christian effort suited to a youth's or child's experience and capacities.[7]

The role of Christian Endeavor for Clark was to train the young people "for Christ and for the church." This would remain the core impulse of the movement throughout his lifetime. This would also guide many of the decisions Clark made in terms of adaptations and organizational adjustments. From the very beginning, Clark saw the training element of Christian Endeavor as unique and sustainable.

When Clark started the first Christian Endeavor Society in Williston, he had an eye on the organization of the society. He realized that if youth were going to be active in ministry in the church, they had to be doing ministry that was significant and that helped the pastor. He also realized that the pastor needed these young people serving and that the young people would need the pastor and some other adults supporting them as they served. These two significant pieces: connection to the

---

7 *Second Annual Conference of the Young People's Society of Christian Endeavor: Held at the Payson Memorial Church, Portland, ME, June 7th, 1883,* 4.

pastor and opportunities to serve, guided the organization of each successful local chapter. For Clark, Christian Endeavor proved a way for all churches to value, train, and engage the young people in the work of the church.

Clark's focus on organizing a specific ministry targeting youth came from the influence of Dr. Theodore Cuyler, the pastor of the Lafayette Avenue Church of Brooklyn. Dr. Cuyler had written an article outlining the importance of an "association" for young people he was experimenting with in his church.[8] While missing the focus on specifically training young people, this idea of associations helped Clark organize a ministry with young people specifically in mind.

From the first society what separated Christian Endeavor was its focus on *training* young people. This was and still remains the heart of the Christian Endeavor Society from the local level to its world-wide organization. Clark understood that many churches were good at instructing youth about Scripture and the Christian life, but the missing link was an opportunity to live it out, to practice implementing it in everyday life.

> "But still there was not in that Church, nor was there in any other church at that time, a sufficient opportunity for young people to express their devotion, or to utilise their enthusiastic love and bounding aspirations in their service of Christ. It was the rarest thing in the world to hear a young voice in the weekly prayer-meeting of the Church, and the very rarity of such an occurrence placed a seal on the lips of most young people."[9]

Training was needed.

---

8 Clark, *The Children and the Church, and the Young People's Society of Christian Endeavor, as a Means of Bringing Them Together.*, 34.

9 Clark, *World Wide Endeavor : The Story of the Young People's Society of Christian Endeavor, from the Beginning and in All Lands*, 54-55; Chaplin, *Francis E. Clark : Founder of the Christian Endeavor Society*, 26.

Christian Endeavor provided each local church with an enormous amount of flexibility in its actions, programs, and events. However there were a few things that Clark saw as essential to keeping the name Christian Endeavor and to finding success in such a society: the Christian Endeavor pledge; the prayer-meeting (also termed the consecration meeting); and the committees. "The essential features, then of the Young People's Society of Christian Endeavor are pledged and constant attendance upon the weekly prayer-meetings, pledged and *constant participation therein by every active member*, pledged and constant work for others, through the committees and in any way which may be suggested."[10]

Clark was influenced by Horace Bushnell's concept of nurture and wanted to create a place for young people to serve. He also realized that young people need to choose for themselves to lead. Clark implemented a two-tiered membership. The active role is for those fully committed to Christ and the church and willing to participate in all activities, especially the weekly prayer meeting. The associate role is for those interested in coming to the activities, but not necessarily willing, yet, to actively participate in the organization of activities or the weekly prayer meeting.[11] This allowed for young people to choose first to be a part of the community and second, to make their faith an active part of their lives.

The Christian Endeavor pledge changed slightly over the years, but its core remained the same:

> Trusting in the Lord Jesus Christ for strength, I promise him that I will strive to whatever he would have me do: that I will make it a rule of mine to pray and read the Bible every day, and to support my own church in every way, especially by attending all her regular Sunday and mid-

10 *Fourth Annual Conference of the Young People's Society of Christian Endeavor: Held at Ocean Park, Old Orchard, Maine, July 8 and 9, 1885, with Papers at the Conference*, 48.

11 Endeavor, *Model Constitution and by-Laws of the Young People's Society of Christian Endeavor*, 3.

Christian Endeavor made an elaborate use of pins and ribbons to represent its many meetings and conventions, and also to encourage members in spiritual growth and outreach. This is a convention pin from the Fifteenth International Convention of Christian Endeavor held in Washington, D.C. in 1896. This convention is also considered the First Convention of World's Christian Endeavor Union.

From the Papers of the International Society of Christian Endeavor in the Archives and Special Collections of B.L. Fisher Library, Asbury Theological Seminary, Wilmore, Kentucky.

week services, unless prevented by some reason which I can conscientiously give to my Savior: and that just as so far I know how, throughout my whole life I will endeavor to lead a Christian life.

As an active member I promise to be true to all my active duties, to be present and take some part, aside from singing, in every Christian Endeavor Prayer Meeting, unless hindered by some reason I can conscientiously give to my Lord and Master. If obliged to be absent from the monthly Consecration Meeting of the Society I will if possible send at least a verse of Scripture to be read in response to my name at the roll call.

The prayer meeting was an integral part of placing leadership on young people from the beginning.

The committee work also gave a place for all young people to significantly contribute to the church and the society. The committees could be easily adapted depending on each local church's needs. New committees could be formed and others could be removed. The important thing was that young people were put in places of leadership to do the work of ministry.

This adaptability of the Christian Endeavor organization was a key part of its sustainability and its effectiveness in so many different cultures. Clark's greatest attribute for the organization may have been his ability to organize the movement as it grew. He continued to adapt and innovate new initiatives as the organization transformed. He responded to requests and needs in the field as well as brought innovation and challenges to fuel the movement's growth. Where many organizational founders fail to stay with the growing needs of an expanding movement, Clark seemed to excel. As Christian Endeavor grew in numbers and spread to other parts of the country, Clark realized the value in gathering together for support and encouragement. To this end he would have groups of societies organize into "unions" by geographic areas. This allowed the groups of people to stay organized and supported, while freeing him up to oversee the continued growth.

Some of the early leaders of the Christian Endeavor Movement: 1. Mr. Anderson, President of the World's Christian Endeavor Convention 2. Mr. Halliwell, 3. Dr. Francis Clark, Founder of Christian Endeavor 4. Mrs. Harriet Clark, or "Mother Clark" 5. Mr. William Shaw, Secretary of the Christian Endeavor Society. While the photo is not dated, it was taken in Jubblupore (Jabalpur), India, which suggests it was taken during the 1909 World's Christian Endeavor Convention in Agra, India.

From the Papers of the International Society of Christian Endeavor in the Archives and Special Collections of B.L. Fisher Library, Asbury Theological Seminary, Wilmore, Kentucky.

Christian Endeavor adapted to different contexts very well. Because it depended only on putting young people into leadership, the model could be used almost anywhere; and it was. From prisons, to boats, to military units, to railroad workers and everywhere in between, Christian Endeavor Societies popped up any place there were groups of young people. Christian Endeavor was also flexible. Soon after its inception there was the development of the Junior Society to help put those younger youth into leadership and ease their transition from Sunday School. Other adaptations included, intermediate societies, alumni groups, devotional emphases, mission initiatives, and family training.

Another significant innovation worth noting was the implementation of the Christian Endeavor Convention. Eighteen months after Clark started the first society, he organized a small gathering to share best practices and encourage churches to continue in training young people. There were six societies and less than 500 people present at the first convention, but it energized the people and help galvanize a movement.[12] The convention idea quickly grew and became an important part of the organization. In addition to annual conventions which would draw people from all over North America and reach over 55,000 attendees, World Wide Conventions were implemented connecting and encouraging Endeavorers from all over the world and catalyzing the continued growth of the movement.

The adaptability of Christian Endeavor at a local level made it a great fit not just in North America, but around the world. The first international society was formed in Hawaii in 1886 (which then was not a state) and from there spread to China and Ceylon (which is now Sri Lanka). Groups of societies were quickly organized into "Unions" and within fourteen years this led to a World Wide Christian Endeavor organization with Dr. Clark as the President and it had its own World Conventions.

---

12 Clark, *Christian Endeavor in All Lands*, 59.

Christian Endeavor spread easily into other English-speaking parts of the world. This is a photo of Margaret Magill (dated 1888), the founder of the Irish Christian Endeavor Society.
From the Papers of the Irish Christian Endeavor Society in the Archives and Special Collections of B.L. Fisher Library, Asbury Theological Seminary, Wilmore, Kentucky.

The American Protestant church of the late 1800's had a problem. Just as the young people of the church were reaching a critical age of in-between Sunday School and church membership, they were experiencing an increasing menu of entertainment options in culture at large. The result was a decrease in Christian faith and church involvement by the young people of the time. Through a commitment to valuing young people, influences from Horace Bushnell and Theodore Cuyler, and adding an emphasis on training, Francis Clark was able to birth the Christian Endeavor Society which provided a solution to the youth problem for both his church and the church at large in the United States and eventually the world. By continuing to innovate, Clark modeled the very flexibility and responsiveness he wished for each local society. He understood that a movement standing still is going backwards, and so his call and his charge was always onward.

Conventions were held all over the world in national societies and for the World Christian Endeavor Union as well. This photo is of a British National Christian Endeavor Convention from 1908.

From the Papers of the World's Christian Endeavor Union in the Archives and Special Collections of B.L. Fisher Library, Asbury Theological Seminary, Wilmore, Kentucky.

Writings of Christian Endeavor

> "There was only one thing to do, and that was to thank God for Guttenberg and the printing-press, and make the most of the printer's ink." - Francis Clark at the 7th Christian Endeavor Convention

One of the factors that led to the rapid spread and growth of Christian Endeavor was the writings of Francis Clark and other leaders. These writings covered the whole scope of literature, from journal articles to song books to travel books and everything in between, and helped get the word out about Christian Endeavor and its new approach to involving youth in the ministry of the church.

Clark was a good writer and wanted to tell people about the success of the Christian Endeavor Society in his own church. He had an awareness that other churches and pastors were trying to reach young people as well, so he shared his idea and the early results. Clark wrote an article about the Christian Endeavor society entitled, "How One Church Looks After Its Young People," that appeared in *The Congregationalist* newspaper.

> "This article, which was merely a brief description of the methods and plans of the Society of Christian Endeavor, now so well known, brought me an unexpected correspondence. I expected to hear no more from this than from any other newspaper article; and, as every

writer knows, that is usually very little. But this article seemed to be on a subject which was exercising the minds of many."[13]

The article was reprinted in *The Sunday-School Times*. "So many were the requests for information that I was soon found necessary to print with a gelantine pad some copies of the constitution which the Williston Society had adopted, to send to inquiring friends."[14] The article and its reprint grabbed the attention of many.

In October 1881, North Church in Newburyport, Massachusetts formed the second society. Rev. Charles Perry Mills in his first year at North Church adopted Christian Endeavor as soon as he heard about it.[15] Newburyport was the first to "second the motion" of Christian Endeavor, but the article Clark wrote reached even further

> "... a pastor in Honolulu placed in his scrap-book an article by Dr. Clark, entitled 'How One Church takes care of its Young People.' This article led the pastor to think that a Christian Endeavor Society would be a good thing for his Church. It was started, and a scrap-book article had led to it. These Honolulu Endeavorers often had passing travelers of different nationalities visiting their meetings, and they in turn carried the seeds of Christian Endeavor to many other places."[16]

Clark was overwhelmed with requests for more information. A year after the formation of the first society, Clark recorded in his journal,

> "It does take a good deal of time to answer all the letters about the Young People's Society but I think it pays. It seems to me I can do more good by working up this method

---

13 Ibid., 53-54.

14 Ibid., 54.

15 Ibid., 57.

16 Chaplin, *Francis E. Clark : Founder of the Christian Endeavor Society*, 49.

of Christian nurture for the young than in any other way. I
am almost ashamed to write so much for the papers about
it but I feel the importance of the subject exceedingly."[17]

After the second society formed, "Demands upon the
parent society and its pastor for information concerning the
work became more and more numerous. A private bureau of
information was practically established, whose expense was
largely divided between Mr. W.H. Pennell, the first signer of
the constitution, and the pastor. The constitution was printed,
and one or two leaflets were prepared to save busy men the
labor of an overburdening correspondence."[18] These leaflets,
copies of the constitution and a few other documents were
copied and sent to those with interest.

Within the first year, three or four societies were added.
In 1882, to add support to the ideas and sparse leaflets about
Christian Endeavor, Clark wrote and published the book, *The
Children and the Church: And the Young Person's Society of
Christian Endeavor As A Means of Bringing Them Together*.
The effectiveness of written communication and the interest
in Christian Endeavor were growing.

As Christian Endeavor grew Clark and the other leaders
realized the need for a publication of their own. Since Christian
Endeavor did not have the financial means to buy a paper, Dr.
Clark and some friends pooled their resources and purchased
The Golden Rule. "Mr. Clark was named the first editor-in-
chief of the paper. Its name was subsequently changed to *The
Christian Endeavor World*, and it attained a circulation of
nearly 100,000."[19] The new paper grew a large audience that
coincided with the growth of the movement becoming one
of the most popular religious weeklies in America. The paper
would also be sent to Christian Endeavorers around the world.
The paper became a vehicle for Clark to do what he seemed

---

17 Clark and Clark, *A Son's Portrait of Dr. Francis E. Clark.*, 80.

18 Clark, *Christian Endeavor in All Lands*, 58.

19 Clark and Clark, *A Son's Portrait of Dr. Francis E. Clark.*, 99.

Dedication of the World Christian Endeavor offices in Boston, Massachusetts, dated July 31, 1918.

From the Papers of the International Society of Christian Endeavor in the Archives and Special Collections of B.L. Fisher Library, Asbury Theological Seminary, Wilmore, Kentucky.

to care for most: help the church. It became a weekly source of encouragement and support, a gathering of best practices, and a reminder for Christian Endeavorers that they were not alone.

The growth of the movement continued. Clark realized very quickly that this manner of "preaching" was effectively a missionary work. Speaking about his first year of Presidency and the issue of handling growth,

> There was only one thing to do, and that was to thank God for Guttenberg and the printing-press, and make the most of the printer's ink. This has been done to the best of our ability; much thought and much time have been put into these publications, and, as a result, in part at least, of those labors, two thousand five hundred and seventy-three societies have been added to the previously long list, an increase in one year of over one hundred per cent. This method of preaching by the use of "white paper and black type" has the advantage of being accurate, swift, capable of reaching an universal audience, and being comparatively inexpensive. One of these missionaries can be equipped and sent, at a moment's notice, to California for two cents, to China for five cents, or to South Africa or Australia for another nickel. These silent missionaries have been nine in number and have been called THE GOLDEN RULE."[20]

Clark was able to utilize this new method of mass media to inform and transform churches and their ministry to young people all over the world.

Clark grew to love these "silent missionaries" and utilized writing throughout his whole life. In looking back at his writing towards the end of his life, Clark notes:

> For more than thirty-five years I have contributed one or more articles and editorials to the Christian Endeavor weekly before mentioned, at least an average of two a

20 *Seventh Annual Conference of the Young People's Society of Christian Endeavor: Held in Battery D Armory, Chicago, Ill., Thursday, Friday, Saturday, and Sunday, July 5,6,7 and 8, 1888, with Papers Read at the Conference*, 51.

Professor Dr. Amos R. Wells (1862-1933), who wrote over 60 books
for the spiritual advancement of the Christian Endeavor Movement,
and who also served as the editor of the *Christian Endeavor World*
from 1891, helped communicate the teachings of the movement
through the print media.
*From the Papers of the International Society of Christian Endeavor
in the Archives and Special Collections of B.L. Fisher Library,
Asbury Theological Seminary, Wilmore, Kentucky.*

week. In the early days of the paper, when I was more responsible for its contents than now, I used to contribute five or six articles, longer or shorter to each issue. When I count up the appalling total of two articles a week for thirty-five years, and fifty-two weeks in the year, I find that the number of contributions amounts to more than 3,600. At least a third as many more must have appeared in other publications of which I can recall at least a score, like *The Christian Herald*, *The Youth's Companion*, and most of the leading denominational papers of American Protestantism.[21]

Clark not only wrote a lot of material, but his writings also covered a large range of styles and topics. He wrote training materials for Christian Endeavor detailing organization and history.[22] He wrote collections of Christian Endeavor stories highlighting some of the "heroes" of the organization's history.[23] He also wrote devotional books to support Christian Endeavor's emphasis on Scripture reading and prayer.[24] He wrote an autobiography at the end of his life, *Memories of Many Men in Many Lands*.[25] In books such as *The Kingdom Within*, he wrote and compiled books that were "selections" from Christian exemplars to help expose young people to a wider range of Christian literature and thought.[26] He wrote largely about and

21 Clark, *Memories of Many Men in Many Lands; an Autobiography*, 673.

22 Francis E. Clark, *The Christian Endeavor Manual : a Text-book on the History, Theory, Principles, and Practice of the Society, with Complete Bibliography and Several Appendixes* (Boston: United Society of Christian Endeavor, 1903); Francis E. Clark, *Young People's Prayer-Meetings in Theory and Practice: With Fifteen Hundred Topics* (New York: Funk & Wagnalls, 1887); Harriet Elizabeth Abbott Clark, *Junior Endeavor in Theory and Practice.* (Andrew Melrose: London, [1904., 1904).

23 Francis E. Clark, *Some Christian Endeavor Saints.* (Boston; Chicago: Congregational Sunday-school and Pub. soc., 1892).

24 John R Clements and Francis E Clark, *Francis E. Clark Year-book: a Collection of Living Paragraphs from Addresses, Books, and Magazine Articles by the Founder of the Young People's Society of Christian Endeavor* (Boston: United Society of Christian Endeavor, 1904).

25 Clark, *Memories of Many Men in Many Lands; an Autobiography*.

26 Francis E Clark, *The Kingdom Within; Selections From the Imitation of Christ* (Boston; Chicago: United Society of Christian Endeavor, 1898).

for Christian Endeavor, but not exclusively. From his travels he recorded travel logs which were widely popular in the United States including *Our Journey Around the World* which went through five editions.[27] He also used the insights gained from travelling to celebrate the culture of recent immigrants to America.[28] In addition to these books, many of the themes and topics of chapters showed up as sermons, articles, and pamphlets.

Christian Endeavor was, of course, more than just Francis Clark. Other leaders wrote extensively about Christian Endeavor as well. These books would cover topics such as methods for running a Christian Endeavor meeting, organizing unions, tributes and histories of the movement, devotional books, Convention reports and even song books. The song books in particular played a very important role in the unification of Christian Endeavor and the propagation of its values.

---

27 Francis E. Clark and Harriet E. Clark, *Our Journey Around the World : an Illustrated Record of a Year's Travel : or Forty Thousand Miles through India, China, Japan, Australia, New Zealand, Egypt, Palestine, Greece, Turkey, Italy, France, Spain, Etc.* (Hartford, Conn.: A.D. Worthington & Co., 1895).

28 Francis E. Clark, *Old Homes of New Americans the Country and the People of the Austro-Hungarian Monarchy and Their Contribution to the New World* (Boston: Houghton Mifflin Co., 1913); Francis E Clark, *Our Italian Fellow Citizens in Their Old Homes and Their New* (New York: Arno Press, 1919).

Impact of Christian Endeavor

"The seed is the Christian Endeavor idea, - small, indeed, at first, and insignificant as a grain of mustard-seed, but potent because in it was the life of God."[29]

What then is the scope of this movement? What is the impact of this society started in a local church, shared by the "traveling missionaries" of Clark's writings, dispersed by Clark's global travels and unified by his organization?

Christian Endeavor's impact can still be felt in the church. First, Christian Endeavor was the first organization to specifically target young people as active and vital contributors to the church. It was the first long-term, effective, age-level specific ministry focused on youth. This specific focus energized a movement that would have significant global impact. The overall scope of Christian Endeavor's effectiveness at energizing young people is probably best shared by Clark himself at the 26th convention:

> At least ten million former members are now active and useful in church-work to a degree far in excess of what would have been their activity without their Christian Endeavor training. There have been at least four million associate members brought to Christ and into church-membership in part through the influence of the society. At least twenty millions of dollars have been given to local church missionary, and charitable objects by Endeavorers.

29 *Seventeenth International Conference of the Young People's Society of Christian Endeavor: Held in the Auditorium Endeavor and Hall Williston, Centennial Park, and in the Gospel Tabernacle and Many Churches*, 62.

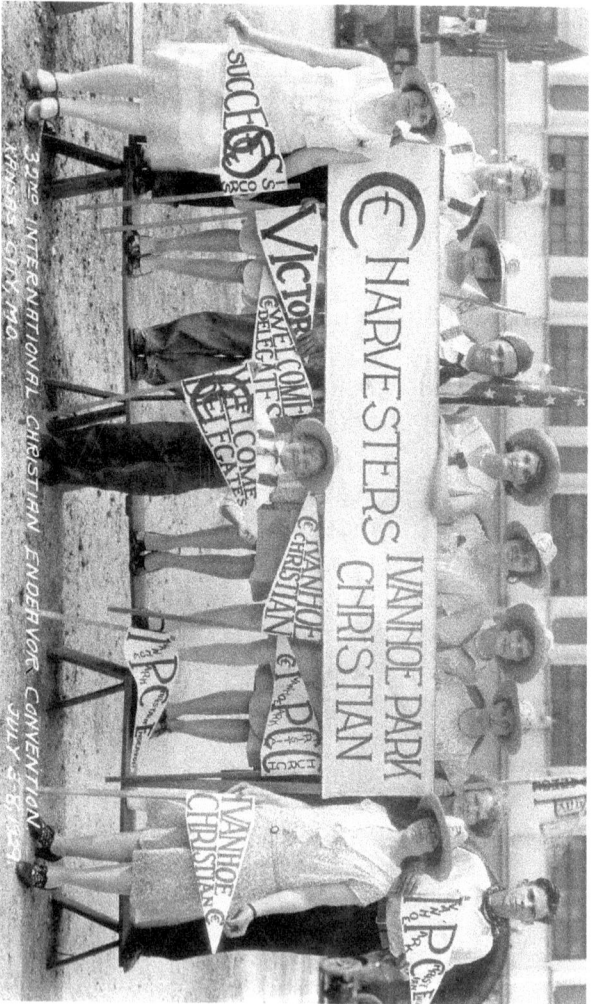

A few of the many delegates to the 32nd Christian Endeavor Convention of 1929 held in Kansas City, Missouri. Delegates often dressed to represent their regions and frequently long parades were held to celebrate the conventions. An astounding 56,425 people attended the largest of the conventions, the 1895 convention in Boston.

From the Papers of the International Society of Christian Endeavor in the Archives and Special Collections of B. L. Fisher Library, Asbury Theological Seminary, Wilmore, Kentucky.

More than fifty millions of young people's meetings have
been held, with an aggregate attendance of at least
one billion five hundred millions. At least one hundred
thousand union meetings and conventions representing all
evangelical denominations have also been held, with an
aggregate attendance of fifty millions, giving a tremendous
impetus toward interdenominational fellowship.[30]

Even more than the numbers of people and dollars, was the
impact:

But who can reckon in millions or billions the amount of
Christly activity in prisons and hospitals, on ships, among
the poor, in fresh-air camps, for Sabbath-observance,
municipal reform, civic betterment, temperance,
social purity, for evangelism, Bible-study, mission-study,
systematic giving, and for international peace and
arbitration? Who can weigh or measure, or tabulate the
religious influence and impulse of these generations of
Christian Endeavorers? I have rehearsed them that we may
record our gratitude to God, and that we may begin our
next generation - get a "running start," as it were, toward
our second three and thirty years with new courage, with
new purposes, with higher aims for a larger and more
substantial advance in all noble-endeavors.[31]

Second, it was important because of its focus on training
youth for the Christian life and leadership through involving
them directly in ministry. It was not seeking to do ministry
for youth, but rather *with* youth. To sum up the heartbeat
and effectiveness of Christian Endeavor, W. Knight Chaplin
writes in his biography of Clark: "The great contribution
which Christian Endeavor has made to the religious life of
this generation has been the development of the personal
responsibility of the young people for their share of the work
and worship of the Church. Thus has it developed men and
women and organizations that have borne the good fruit."[32]

---

30 *Twenty-Sixth International Christian Endeavor Convention: Held in
Fiesta Park, The Temple Beautiful, and in Many Churches, Los Angeles,
California*, July 9-14, 1913, 38.

31 Ibid.

32 Chaplin, *Francis E. Clark : Founder of the Christian Endeavor Society,*

Due to its size and influence with young people, Christian Endeavor came to exert considerable political influence. Numerous presidents of the United States were affiliated with Christian Endeavor and sent greetings to national conventions. In 1911, President William Taft became the only U.S. President to address an annual Christian Endeavor Convention while in office, when he spoke at the Atlantic City Convention in New Jersey. This image shows a meal with President Taft, Francis Clark and other Christian Endeavor and political leaders after Taft's speech at the convention. Both Presidents Richard Nixon and Ronald Reagan did their first public speaking as young members of Christian Endeavor societies.

From the Papers of the International Society of Christian Endeavor in the Archives and Special Collections of B.L. Fisher Library, Asbury Theological Seminary, Wilmore, Kentucky.

And again: "Christian Endeavor at its best is a great educator because it inaugurates a leading-out process of the religious life of young people. It discovers a young person to himself as well as to others. It shows him that he has a tongue to be used in speaking of Jesus, and hands to be used in working for Him, and feet for running His errands, and, above all, a heart for loving Him supremely."[33] The church would never be the same because of Christian Endeavor's focus specifically on ministry *with* youth. This focus allowed Christian Endeavor to be a developer of Christian leaders within the church but also within society. Christian Endeavor has left a lasting impact on the global Protestant church.

118.
33 Ibid., 119-120.

Often referred to as "Father Clark" and "Mother Clark," Frances Clark (1851-1927) and his wife, Harriet (Abbott) Clark (1850-1945) were often the face of Christian Endeavor. Harriet would develop the model on which Junior Christian Endeavor was developed for younger children, and later be recognized as a co-founder with her husband. The two remained involved in the movement throughout their lives.

From the Papers of the International Society of Christian Endeavor in the Archives and Special Collections of B.L. Fisher Library, Asbury Theological Seminary, Wilmore, Kentucky.

Leaders of Christian Endeavor

Francis Clark (1851-1927)

Francis Clark was the founder and organizer of Christian Endeavor. He became the President of the United Society of Christian Endeavor in 1888 and remained in that role until he resigned in 1925. He was elected President of the World Wide Society of Christian Endeavor when it was formed in 1895 and held that title until his death in 1927. Despite his many accomplishments in those roles, he had a strong group of other leaders who helped to grow and continue Christian Endeavor.

Harriett Clark (1850-1945)

Often referred to as "Mother Christian Endeavor," Harriett Clark was a vital part of the success of her husband, Francis Clark, and Christian Endeavor. Harriett Abbott and Francis Clark met while Francis was a student at Andover Seminary. The Abbott family home was a place of help and refuge for many a seminarian and when Francis Clark was getting ready to graduate, having spent a lot of time with the Abbotts; it was no surprise that he asked Harriett to marry him.

Harriett was a direct descendant of the Pilgrim, John Alden, who was came to America on the *Mayflower*.[34] She was strong of character and determination. William Shaw, who was one of her students writes, "Slender and spirituelle in appearance, she looked as if a strong breeze would blow her away. But in that little body there was an indomitable will,

---

34 Shaw, *The Evolution of an Endeavorer*, 56.

as the experiences of fifty years have abundantly proved."[35] She was a school teacher and was happy to serve children and youth. She met Francis while they were both serving young people at a mission Sunday School. This would set the tone for the rest of their lives.

Harriett had a great ministry in her own right, caring for Junior Christian Endeavor leaders for the last half of her life. She was a favorite speaker, especially at missionary gatherings. She was also a writer, often assisting Francis in his work and co-authoring one of their travel books, *Our Journey Around the World*. She helped write articles and editorials for *The Christian Endeavor World* as well. She traveled often with her husband on his many journeys around the world carrying her portable typewriter so she could transcribe her husband's writings.

She and Dr. Clark had five children, two daughters and three sons, whom she raised, taught, and cared for. She revised the saying due to her ability to knit almost anywhere, "This one thing I do," to instead say, "These two things I do at one and the same time."[36]

Amos Wells (1862-1933)

Another of the more influential leaders in Christian Endeavor was Amos Russel Wells. A professor at Antioch College, Ohio, Wells had a significant role in leading and organizing Christian Endeavor. As William Shaw, General Secretary for Christian Endeavor, notes, "Next to Dr. Clark, to Professor Wells belongs the credit of having contributed more of real and permanent value to Christian Endeavor than any other person connected with the movement. The Christian Endeavor idea was born in the brain and heart of Dr. Clark, and its principles and spiritual possibilities have had no abler exponent; but to Professor Wells was given the task of formulating its methods and outlining its

---

35 Ibid.

36 Ibid., 58.

plans of service."[37] Wells was a very capable author with over 63 books published on topics varying from poetry to Christian Endeavor organization to the role of young people in the church. An early and frequent contributor to *The Golden Rule* (which later became *The Christian Endeavor World*), Wells became that magazine's editor in 1891 and the editor of *The Junior Gold Rule* in 1893. He was also editor of *Peloubet's Notes on the International Sunday-School Lessons*. Wells grew up in Christian Endeavor and under Dr. Clark's leadership became a most recognized leader himself.

William Shaw (1860-1941)

It is hard to imagine the story of Christian Endeavor without mentioning William Shaw. He was the driving force behind the business side of Christian Endeavor. He is a great representation of so many Endeavorers. He was born in a humble home, had very little opportunities for formal education, and yet found in Christian Endeavor a chance to develop, learn, grow, contribute, and lead.

He grew up in a Christian home, but did not fully commit his life to Christ until he was eighteen. He immediately was put into leadership in the Sunday School at that church. His whole life he was naturally curious, always interested in reading and learning from those wiser than he. He took this to his new life in Christ, and while never a great student in school became a constant learner.

He first met Dr. Clark when Shaw's church, Phillips Church in Boston, called Clark to be its pastor. He was thrilled to discover that Clark's wife, Harriett, had been one of his grammar school teachers before she was married. In Phillips Church, Clark started a Young Person's Society of Christian Endeavor and

Shaw attended the weekly Tuesday night meetings. Because of Dr. Clark's energy and organization, Shaw was eager to be a

---

37 Ibid., 72-73.

From North
來 北 從

From West   From Sinim
來 西 從   來 國 秦 從
Come Over   Help Us

C E

All Within

Four Seas

Brethren

第 兄 海 四

來 南 從

From Far

Early on various national societies would send or bring banners to represent their nations at International Conventions held in the United States. This is a hand painted silk banner sent from Chinese Christian Endeavor societies to one such early convention. In 1899 there were 148 Christian Endeavor Societies in China.

From the Papers of the International Society of Christian Endeavor in the Archives and Special Collections of B.L. Fisher Library, Asbury Theological Seminary, Wilmore, Kentucky.

part and quickly became the first President of the society and a recognized leader.

In 1886 Clark asked Shaw to take on the role of Treasurer for the United Society of Christian Endeavor (then the overarching organizing body). A short time later Christian Endeavor purchased a paper to help with its work, and Shaw quit his job at the carpet store and became the Advertising Manager of *The Golden Rule*. As Christian Endeavor continued to grow and the success of *The Golden Rule* grew, the leaders of Christian Endeavor realized the need for more publications of books, leaflets, and general literature. Shaw was chosen in 1889 to be the Publication Manager to develop the publication department for the United Society. Still in these capacities as Treasurer of the United Society and publication manager, in 1895 Shaw saw the World's Christian Endeavor Union organized and he was elected treasurer. In 1898 Shaw was asked to become the business manager for *The Christian Endeavor World* (formerly *The Golden Rule*) because of its financial condition. He moved into that role from publication manager and returned the paper to a strong financial foundation. In 1910, Shaw would return to publication manager and began serving as general secretary for the United Society.

Daniel Poling (1884-1968)

Dr. Clark's successor as President of the International Christian Endeavor and the World Christian Endeavor was Daniel A. Poling. Poling first encountered Christian Endeavor as a member of the Junior Society of Christian Endeavor in Lafayette, Oregon, and served Christian Endeavor the rest of his life. He quickly fell in love with Christian Endeavor because of its impact on his own life and because of its work around the world. He was active in serving the church, joined the Student Volunteer Movement, and was planning on serving in China. Just before he left, his trunk packed with all of his belongings already enroute, his denomination, United Evangelical, called him to be a recruiter in the United States of young people for

"Mother Clark" with Dr. Daniel Poling and his wife Susan (Vandersall) Poling at the 32nd International Christian Endeavor Convention in 1929 in Kansas City, Missouri. Dr. Poling was the second president of the International Society of Christian Endeavor (1925-1949 and 1954-1955) and of the World's Union of Christian Endeavor (1927-1962), taking over from Francis Clark.

From the Papers of the International Society of Christian Endeavor in the Archives and Special Collections of B.L. Fisher Library, Asbury Theological Seminary, Wilmore, Kentucky.

missionary work.[38]

He moved to Columbus, Ohio to continue his studies and there became the field secretary of the Ohio Christian Endeavor Union. It was in this role that Poling first encountered Dr. Clark in 1909 at the Ohio State Christian Endeavor Convention. Poling writes of the encounter, "I came immediately under his spell. A benign, considerate, thoughtful personality, an inspirational speaker, and a fine administrator, he encouraged my interest in young people's religious activities, and I in turn saw the possibilities in his international, interdenominational Christian Endeavor movement."[39] Clark must have been impressed by Poling as well, because shortly after that meeting Poling was summoned by Clark to the Christian Endeavor headquarters in Boston. Poling gained more and more responsibility until he was elected president of the International Society in 1925 and was named president of the World's Christian Endeavor Union in 1927.

Poling is known for carrying Christian Endeavor with him wherever he went. He was involved in many roles and activities outside of Christian Endeavor as well. He pastored several churches including the Marble Collegiate Dutch Reformed Church in New York City and the Baptist Temple in Philadelphia. While serving at the Baptist Temple, his son, Clark, was killed in the war while serving as a chaplain on the *Dorchester*. Clark Poling along with three other chaplains on the boat helped organize the evacuation and when needed gave up their own life jackets so others could live. Daniel Poling helped to build and then pastor the Chapel of the Four Chaplains, an interfaith chapel honoring these four men.

Poling, like his predecessor, was a writer as well as a leader. He authored twenty-five books in his lifetime including four novels. Many of these books were about Christian Endeavor. He was the editor of *The Christian Herald*, a popular non-

---

38 Ibid., 100.

39 Pagel, Arno, *Worldwide Christian Endeavor*, 12.

denominational Protestant journal and helped it grow in popularity and subscriptions.[40] He served on the editorial board for *The Christian Endeavor World*. He was also able to use his writings to leverage influence for young people, the church, and Christian Endeavor.

Daniel Poling served his country as well. He was a leader in the Prohibition movement eventually becoming the Prohibition Party's nominee for Governor of Ohio in 1912. During World War I, he was a chaplain for Christian Endeavor and the Y.M.C.A. in France. While taking supplies to some of the young men on the front lines he was gassed. Poling survived the attack, but was physically impacted for the rest of his life.[41] For his work he was the first clergyman to receive the Medal of Merit, the highest civilian award given by his country at that time. In his role as Christian Endeavor president, Poling knew many influential people and was tabbed by President Harry S. Truman to help investigate the United States Steel Company Strike.[42] He was also active in the anti-communist movement.

It must be noted that throughout all of Daniel Poling's life and work, he was a committed advocate of young people and Christian Endeavor. "Dr. Dan," as his friends called him, worked hard in the midst of a world in crisis with two World Wars to help young people serve Christ and the Church.

---

40 Ibid., 14.

41 Shaw, *The Evolution of an Endeavorer*, 101.

42 Ibid.

Growth and Decline of Christian Endeavor

The growth of Christian Endeavor was remarkable. In 1882 there were seven known societies. In 1883 there were 56. Growth continued to 156 societies in 1884. In 1886 there were 850 societies, representing eight denominations, thirty-three states and seven foreign countries. In 1887, only six years after starting, over seven thousand societies were reported with over half a million members. Five years later, in 1892 there were 21,080 societies. By 1902 there were 52,000 societies and nearly three and three-quarter million members representing all of the United States and forty-one foreign countries. In 1913 the five million member mark was surpassed. In 1921 the society reported 80,000 societies covering the world![43] What led to this enormous growth and impact? Dr. Clark's work cannot be overlooked. He was a great leader and writer, and through his global travels to conventions, he was a present encourager of Christian Endeavor and its value of young people.

Dr. Clark himself attributed the growth of Christian Endeavor to two things other than himself: the people and God's work. It is interesting that while Clark did take Christian Endeavor and its ideals with him all over the world, traveling around the world four different times, he often found when he arrived places that Christian Endeavor was already there.

---

43 The numbers listed are gathered from the following two sources as well as Convention reports from the various years, Clark, *Christian Endeavor in All Lands*; Clark, *Training the Church of the Future*; *Auburn Seminary Lectures on Christian Nurture with Special Reference to the Young People's Society of Christian Endeavor as a Training-school of the Church*.

Der Reichspräsident   Berlin, den 5. August 1930.

Brieftelegramm.

Den in Berlin zu ihrer 8.Welttagung versammelten
Vertretern des Jugendbundes für entschiedenes Christentum
entbiete ich herzliche Willkommengrüsse. Ich verbinde damit
meine besten Wünsche für einen gesegneten Erfolg ihrer
Tagung und ihrer Arbeit zur Verbreitung christlicher Gesin-
nung.

von Hindenburg (signature)

TRANSLATION

To the representatives of the Young People's Society of Christian
Endeavor, assembled in Berlin for their eighth World's Convention,
I send hearty welcome-greetings. I extend also my best wishes
for blessing and success both of your convention and also of your
work in spreading the Christian spirit.

von Hindenburg

(President of the German Republic)

An die   To the

Welttagung des Jugendbundes für   World Convention of the Young

entschiedenes Christentum,   People's Society of Christian

Berlin-Funkhaus.   Endeavor.

**A telegram welcoming delegates to the eighth World's Christian
Endeavor Convention in Berlin, Germany in 1930 from the German
President, Paul Von Hindenburg. The World's Christian Endeavor
Union formed in 1895 at the Boston International Christian
Endeavor and by 1899 there were 10,000 societies in 49 different
nations.**

*From the Papers of the World's Christian Endeavor Union
in the Archives and Special Collections of B.L. Fisher Library,
Asbury Theological Seminary, Wilmore, Kentucky.*

As Clark traveled he would often visit missionaries who had taken Christian Endeavor from the United States and began to implement it wherever they were sent. Clark was aware that American missionaries and other churchmen were incredibly helpful in spreading Christian Endeavor globally. Christian Endeavor was always a supporter of missions so this led to a natural sending of many Christian Endeavorers into the field.

The first article that Clark wrote about Christian Endeavor made its way into the hands of a pastor in Honolulu, Hawaii. This was a major hub for travel to the East from America. From there many a church leader, missionary, and layperson observed Christian Endeavor and took it with them to the East.

> A missionary took Christian Endeavor to China. The Rev. George H. Hubbard, of Foochow, could not see why the Movement should not be just as good for China as he had found it in America, so he organized a society in a Church at Foochow. The first Chinese Endeavourer was Mr. Ling, who said in an address at a Convention in Shanghai that the object of their Christian Endeavor Society was 'to drive the devil out of China.' They have not wholly succeeded in doing that yet, but all over China over 2,500 societies are doing something towards it. There is now a United Society for all China. The first society in Foochow was called by a Chinese word which means "The Drum and Rouse-up Society" - not a bad translation of Christian Endeavor.[44]

Because Christian Endeavor was so adaptable and helpful for the church, it became an indigenous movement wherever it went, being adopted and adapted by local leaders for the good of the Church. Its dissemination was not accomplished by just one person or one specific strategy, but by an army of men and women set on helping young people lead.

The other factor that Clark attributes to the growth and spread of the movement is God's provision. In his autobiography, Clark

---

[44] Chaplin, Francis E. Clark : *Founder of the Christian Endeavor Society*, 50.

Christian Endeavor has spread all over the world, and continues to be active in numerous nations. This photo is of a 1956 conference of the World's Christian Endeavor Union for the Asia Pacific region, held in Karuizwa, Japan.

From the Papers of the World's Christian Endeavor Union in the Archives and Special Collections of B.L. Fisher Library, Asbury Theological Seminary, Wilmore, Kentucky is clear about where the credit for the movement's success should go:

> I am particularly impressed in my devotional moments with God's undeserved goodness in giving me my special work in the world. Realizing my Lamentations of intellect and soul, I wonder that He called me to start, and in some measure to develop, the work of the Christian Endeavor society. I see hundreds of my brother ministers more eloquent, more witty, more gifted in many ways than I. Why were they not chosen? Thousands of them were thinking along the same lines of Christian nurture in the early eighties. Why did He not give this honor to one of them? Why was the little experiment in Williston Church His chosen way of influencing millions in all lands for good?
>
> This is no mock humility. The undeserved eulogies with which I am sometimes introduced on the platform, often make me cringe and cover my face, for I realize, as no one else can, how small has really been my part, and how all-embracing God's part has been in fitting the cause to the time, and in commissioning a multitude of young men and women for the special tasks He has given them through Christian Endeavor. Every month He has opened new doors; every month He has called young leaders to enter them, and they have responded, "Lord, here am I, send me!"[45]

Christian Endeavor reached its peak numbers in the 1920's. Its numeric decline can be attributed to a number of factors including the death of Francis Clark and thus the end of his gifted leadership, the growth of denominational youth organizations which targeted the same audience, and the World Wars which involved the focus and the lives of many young men and women. As has been highlighted above, Clark was an incredible leader who somehow managed to lead a rapidly growing International Christian Endeavor society (called "International" first because it included Canada) and, later, the World Wide Christian Endeavor society. His ability to adapt his leadership to suit these two organizations as

---

45 Clark, *Memories of Many Men in Many Lands : An Autobiography*, 691-692.

Portrait of Francis E. Clark.
From the Papers of the International Society of Christian Endeavor in the Archives and Special Collections of B.L. Fisher Library, Asbury Theological Seminary, Wilmore, Kentucky.

their needs grew and changed is remarkable, not to mention his unique ability to write and speak in such a personal way. Anyone following as the President of those societies had huge shoes to fill and it is not a critique of a specific leader that makes this transition so significant.

Before Clark and Christian Endeavor, there was very little focus on or room for youth in the church aside from patiently observing ministry until they reached adulthood. After Christian Endeavor was born and modeled a successful way of reaching and training young people, churches began to adopt Christian Endeavor or "borrowed" the idea. Denominations in particular liked the idea so much that they took the principle of having an age specific ministry to young people and adapted it to their denominations. In so doing they created an avenue to propagate denominational literature and curriculum that communicated the importance of denominational values. This started with only a few denominations at first, but gradually grew until by the middle of the 20th century, almost all denominations had their own youth ministry literature and curriculum as well as denominational leaders to guide local churches in this ministry to youth.

Some denominations wanted to do this while Clark was alive, but he adamantly fought against it, arguing, successfully in most cases, for unity in the church. When Clark passed away, his relationships with denominational leaders went with him, and denominations coupled this desire with stronger infrastructures and more resources to move forward with their own youth ministry programs and agendas.

The global political climate also played a role in the downturn in Christian Endeavor societies and members. The world twice went to war. This not only stopped communication and travel to many parts of the world, but it also occupied the resources and attention of many young men and women. The church as a whole struggled to focus on anything but surviving the wars and Christian Endeavor, while always active in supporting and propagating unity and peace, felt the effects of the wars as well.

In the second half of the twentieth century, Christian Endeavor had many unions and societies close down. An effort to combine Christian Endeavor with denominational youth groups in one united organization was not successful. The memory of the effectiveness of Christian Endeavor and its training model were largely forgotten as many youth have never experienced either.

Currently, Christian Endeavor still exists and still has the purpose of training young people for leadership in the church. The Worldwide Christian Endeavor has headquarters in Germany and is continuing to resource the societies that exist in the world at large. The International Society has moved its headquarters to Edmore, Michigan and is experiencing some growth and revitalization as churches and ministries learn about the mission of Christian Endeavor. In a religious climate that is moving away from denominational structures and is again desperate to reach youth, Christian Endeavor is providing much needed resource for the church in training young people.

Works Cited

Chaplin, W. Knight. *Francis E. Clark : Founder of the Christian Endeavor Society*. London: British Christian Endeavor Union, 1900.

Clark, Eugene Francis, and Sydney Clark. *A Son's Portrait of Dr. Francis E. Clark*. Boston: Williston Press, 1930.

Clark, Francis E. *Christian Endeavor in All Lands*. Philadelphia: n.p., 1906.

——. *Memories of Many Men in Many Lands : An Autobiography*. Boston; Chicago: United Society of Christian Endeavor, 1923.

—— . *The Children and the Church, and the Young People's Society of Christian Endeavor, as a Means of Bringing Them Together*. Boston: Congregational Sunday School and Pub. society, 1882.

—— . *World Wide Endeavor: The Story of the Young People's Society of Christian Endeavor, from the Beginning and in All Lands*. Philadelphia: Gillespie, 1895.

Endeavor, Young People's Society of Christian. *Model Constitution and by-Laws of the Young People's Society of Christian Endeavor*. Toronto: Endeavor Herald, 1898.

Fourth Annual Conference of the Young People's Society of Christian Endeavor: Held at Ocean Park, Old Orchard, Maine, July 8 and 9, 1885, with Papers at the Conference. Lynn, Mass.: Lewis & Winship Printers, 1885.

Pagel, Arno. *Worldwide Christian Endeavor*. Columbus, Ohio: World's Christian Endeavor Union, 1981.

Second Annual Conference of the Young People's Society of Christian Endeavor: Held at the Payson Memorial Church, Portland, ME, June 7th, 1883. Burlington, Vermont: H.S. Styles, Steam Book and Job Printer, 1883.

Seventeenth International Conference of the Young People's Society of Christian Endeavor: Held in the Auditorium Endeavor and Hall Williston, Centennial Park, and in the Gospel Tabernacle and Many Churches. Boston: United Society of Christian Endeavor, 1898.

Seventh Annual Conference of the Young People's Society of Christian Endeavor: Held in Battery D Armory, Chicago, Ill., Thursday, Friday, Saturday, and Sunday, July 5,6,7 and 8, 1888, with Papers Read at the Conference. Boston, MA: The United Society of Christian Endeavor, 1888.

Shaw, William. *The Evolution of an Endeavorer: An Autobiography*. Boston, Massachusetts: Christian Endeavor World, 1924.

Springhall, John. "Building Character in the British Boy: The Attempt to Extend Christian Manliness to Working-Class Adolescents, 1880-1914." edited by J. A. Mangan and James Walvin. Manliness and Morality : Middle-Class Masculinity in Britain and America, 1800-1940. New York: St. Martin's Press, 1987.

Twenty-Sixth International Christian Endeavor Convention: Held in Fiesta Park, The Temple Beautiful, and in Many Churches, Los Angeles, California, July 9-14, 1913. Boston: United Society of Christian Endeavor, 1913.

www.ingramcontent.com/pod-product-compliance
Lightning Source LLC
Chambersburg PA
CBHW060617030426
42337CB00018B/3097